Hurricane Ian: A Warning from the Future

Introduction

This book tells the story of Hurricane Ian, from its origin to landfall to its aftermath. It also provides valuable information on how to prepare for and stay safe during hurricanes.

Learn how Hurricane Ian formed and why it became such a powerful storm. We also discuss the factors that had a devastating impact on Florida.

We will provide a detailed report on Hurricane Ian's landfall and its aftermath. We cover the damage caused by the storm, the loss of life, and the heroic efforts of first responders and volunteers.

We provide valuable information to help you prepare and stay safe during a hurricane. Topics include evacuation planning, emergency preparedness kits, and home safety measures.

We hope this book helps you understand the power and destructive potential of hurricanes. We also hope it provides you with the information you need to stay safe during the next hurricane.

Table of contents

What to pack in your emergency bag?

How to protect your home and property?

Where would you go if you needed to evacuate?

How to stay safe during a hurricane?

What should I do if I'm stuck at home during a hurricane?

How to recover from a hurricane?

How to assess damage to your home and property?

How to make an insurance claim?

How to get help from FEMA and other organisations?

Lessons learned from Hurricane Ian

Preparing for the next hurricane

Hurricane Ian Case Study: Stories of those affected by the storm

Hurricane preparedness tips for specific populations, including seniors, people with disabilities, and pets

List of resources for hurricane relief and recover

Chapter 1

What is Hurricane Ian?

Hurricane Ian is a powerful and destructive Category 4 Atlantic hurricane that struck Florida in September 2023. With an estimated loss of $112 billion, it was the third costliest weather disaster in U.S. history. Ian was also the deadliest hurricane to hit Florida since the 1935 Labour Day Hurricane, and the deadliest hurricane to hit Florida since Michael in 2018.

• Education and Development •

Ian originated from a tropical wave that appeared off the coast of West Africa on September 19th. The wave moved westward in the Atlantic Ocean, gradually developing into a tropical cyclone, which became a tropical cyclone on September 23. Ian rapidly strengthened over the next few days, reaching hurricane strength on September 25th. On September 27, Ian strengthened into a Category 4 hurricane, with maximum sustained winds of 255 mph.

• Landing and impact •

 Ian made landfall near Cayo Costa, Florida on September 28th. The storm weakened slightly as it passed through the state, but remained a strong hurricane. Ian surfaced in the Atlantic Ocean on 29 September and continued tracking north. The storm strengthened again on September 30, becoming a Category 1 hurricane, before making landfall in Georgetown, South Carolina. Ian weakened as it moved inland through South Carolina and North Carolina, becoming a tropical storm. The storm subsided in south western Virginia on October 1st.

 Ian caused widespread damage and flooding in Florida, South Carolina, and North Carolina. Storm surge reached up to 18 feet in some areas, and heavy rain caused widespread river flooding. Ian also caused widespread power outages and damage to infrastructure.

• Damage and loss of life •

 The death toll from Hurricane Ian is estimated at more than 150. Most of the deaths occurred in Florida, with some deaths also reported in South Carolina and North Carolina.

 Ian caused an estimated $112 billion in damage, making it the third costliest weather disaster in U.S. history. Damage was concentrated in Florida, but significant damage was also reported in South Carolina and North Carolina.

 Hurricane Ian was a devastating storm that caused significant damage and deaths. The storm's impact highlights the importance of preparing for hurricanes and other natural disasters.

Chapter 2
How did Hurricane Ian occur?

Hurricane Ian formed in the central tropical Atlantic Ocean from a tropical wave that emerged from the coast of West Africa on September 19, 2023. The wave moved westward across the Atlantic Ocean, gradually developing into a tropical depression and then a tropical storm on September 23. Ian strengthened rapidly over the next few days, reaching hurricane status on September 25.

The conditions that were favourable for Hurricane Ian's formation and development included:

• Warm ocean waters: Hurricanes need warm ocean waters to form and develop. The ocean waters in the central tropical Atlantic Ocean were very warm in September 2023, which provided the energy that Ian needed to strengthen.

• Low wind shear: Wind shear is the change in wind direction and speed with altitude. High wind shear can disrupt the development of hurricanes. However, the wind shear in the central tropical Atlantic Ocean was low in September 2023, which allowed Ian to strengthen.

• Favourable atmospheric conditions: The atmospheric conditions in the central tropical Atlantic Ocean were also favourable for Hurricane Ian's development. There was a strong upper-level ridge of high pressure over the region, which provided a favourable steering environment for the storm.

Ian strengthened rapidly due to the favourable conditions in the central tropical Atlantic Ocean. The storm reached Category 4 hurricane status on September 27, with maximum sustained winds of 155 mph. Ian made landfall near Cayo Costa, Florida, on September 28 as a Category 4 hurricane.

It is important to note that climate change is likely making hurricanes more intense and destructive. Warmer ocean waters provide more energy for hurricanes to develop and strengthen. Additionally, climate change is causing sea levels to rise, which means that storm surges from hurricanes can reach higher levels and cause more damage.

Hurricane Ian is a reminder of the importance of being prepared for hurricanes and other natural disasters. It is important to have a plan in place in case of a hurricane, and to know what to do if a hurricane is approaching your area.

Chapter 3

Why is Hurricane Ian so strong?

Here's why Hurricane Ian is so strong.

Warm ocean water: Warm ocean water is required for hurricane formation and development. In September 2023, the waters of the central tropical Atlantic Ocean were so warm that they provided Ian with the energy he needed to sustain life.

Low Wind Shear: Wind shear is the change in wind direction and speed with altitude. Strong wind shear can hinder hurricane development. However, in September 2023, wind shear in the central tropical Atlantic was low, allowing Ian to strengthen.

Favourable Atmospheric Conditions: Atmospheric conditions in the tropical mid-Atlantic were also favourable for the development of Hurricane Ian. A strong upper-level ridge of anticyclone existed in this region, providing a favourable control environment for the storm.

In addition to these factors, climate change could make hurricanes more powerful and destructive. Warmer ocean waters provide more energy for hurricane development and strengthening. Additionally, climate change is causing sea levels to rise, meaning storm surges from hurricanes can reach higher levels and cause more damage. Below is a detailed explanation of each factor that contributed to Hurricane Ian's strength.

Warm ocean water: Hurricanes are powered by latent heat of evaporation from the ocean surface. As the ocean warms, more water evaporates, providing more energy for hurricanes. Hurricane Ian formed in September 2023 over the central tropical Atlantic Ocean, where ocean waters were very warm. This warm water provided Ian with the energy he needed to quickly strengthen himself. Low

Wind Shear: Wind shear is the change in wind direction and speed with altitude. Strong wind shear can tear hurricanes apart and hinder their development. However, wind shear in the tropical central Atlantic in September 2023 was low, allowing Ian to strengthen unhindered.

Favourable Atmospheric Conditions: Atmospheric conditions in the tropical mid-Atlantic were also favourable for the development of Hurricane Ian. A strong upper-level ridge of anticyclone existed in this area. This ridge of high pressure provided a favourable environment for the storm, steering it west toward Florida. Due to warmer ocean temperatures and rising sea levels, climate change could make hurricanes stronger and more destructive. Warmer ocean waters provide more energy for hurricane development and strengthening. Additionally, rising sea levels mean storm surges from hurricanes can reach higher levels and cause more damage.

Chapter 4

Where is Hurricane Ian headed

Hurricane Ian dissipated in south-western Virginia on October 1, 2023. It's no longer a threat.

However, it is important to note that the Atlantic hurricane season runs from June 1st to November 30th. Even without Ian, there's still a chance of more hurricanes this season. It's important to stay up to date with the latest weather forecasts and warnings from the National Hurricane Centre. If you live in a hurricane-prone area, it's important to have a plan in place in case a hurricane occurs. This plan should include:

- Know where to go if you need to evacuate

- Prepare an emergency response kit with food, water, and other essentials

- Ensure the safety of your home and property

By planning, you can protect yourself and your loved ones from the dangers of a hurricane.

Chapter 5

What are the possible impacts of Hurricane Ian?

Hurricane Ian is a powerful and destructive storm that can have significant impacts on areas in its path. These effects include:

Storm Surge: Storm surge is the abnormal rise in sea level that occurs along coastlines during hurricanes. Storm surges can inundate coastal areas, causing flooding and damage to property and infrastructure. Hurricane Ian is expected to cause storm surges of up to 18 feet in some areas.

Heavy Rain: Hurricane Ian is expected to produce heavy rain that could cause flash flooding and river flooding. Flash floods can occur unexpectedly, rapidly, and can be life-threatening. River flooding can cause widespread damage to property and infrastructure.

High Winds: Hurricane Ian is expected to produce strong winds that could damage or destroy trees, power lines, and other structures. Strong winds may also make travel difficult and may cause power outages.

Tornados: Hurricanes can also produce tornadoes. Tornadoes are rotating columns of air that can cause significant damage.

In addition to these physical effects, Hurricane Ian could also have a significant impact on people's lives. Hurricane Ian can cause:

Loss of life: Hurricane Ian is a dangerous storm that can lead to loss of life. It is important to follow instructions from local authorities and evacuate if instructed to do so.

Injuries: Hurricane Ian can cause injuries from flying debris, strong winds, and storm surge. It is important to take precautions to protect yourself and your loved ones from injury.

Property Damage: Hurricane Ian could cause significant property damage due to storm surge, high winds, and flooding. It is important to have a plan in place to protect your property from damage.

Power Outages: Hurricane Ian could cause power outages due to damage to power lines. Power outages can make it difficult to obtain information about the storm and access critical services.

Critical Services Disruption: Hurricane Ian could impact critical services such as water, wastewater, transportation, and communications services. This disorder can make it difficult to meet basic needs.

It is important to prepare for the potential impacts of Hurricane Ian. You need to plan for your family and estate. Also check out the latest weather forecasts and warnings from the National Hurricane Centre. If you are in an area at risk for Hurricane Ian, you should follow these steps to prepare.

• Know your evacuation zones and plan where to go if you need to evacuate.

• Create an emergency kit with food, water, and other essentials.

• Keep your home and property safe.

• Stay up to date with the latest weather forecasts and warnings from the National Hurricane Centre.

These are some steps you can take to protect yourself and your loved ones from the dangers of Hurricane Ian.

Chapter 6

What should I do to prepare for Hurricane Ian

Here are some steps you can take to prepare for Hurricane Ian.

• Before the storm •

• Know your evacuation zones and plan where to go if you need to evacuate.

• Evacuation zones can be found on your local emergency management agency's website.

• Create an emergency kit containing food, water, and other essentials

• Kits must contain enough food and water for at least 3 days for each person in the household. You should also bring other essentials such as a first aid kit, flashlight, batteries, radio, and medication. • Keep your home and property safe.

• Board up windows and doors and cut down trees and branches that could fall and damage your home. If you have time, you can also equip your property with sandbags to protect it from flooding.

• Stay informed about the latest weather forecasts and warnings from the National Hurricane Centre.

• You can monitor the latest weather information on the National Hurricane Centre website or on your local news station.

• During the storm •

• If you are ordered to evacuate, do so immediately.

• Do not delay evacuating until it is too late.

• If you are unable to evacuate, stay indoors and go to a room on the lowest level of your home.

• If your home has a basement, go to the basement.

• Stay away from windows and doors.

• Listen to the radio for updates on the storm.

• After the storm •

• Do not go outside until the storm has completely passed.

• Check for damage to your home and property.

• If your home is damaged, contact your insurance company to file a claim.

• Stay informed about the latest information on recovery efforts.

Here are some additional tips for preparing for Hurricane Ian:

• Make sure you have a plan for your pets.

• If you need to evacuate, you will need to make arrangements for your pets to be cared for.

• Have a plan for communicating with family and friends during the storm.

• Cell phone service may be disrupted during a hurricane, so it is important to have a backup plan for communicating.

• Be prepared for power outages.

• Prepare a flashlight, batteries, and radio in case of a power outage.

• Be prepared for flooding.

• If you live in a flood-prone area, bring sandbags and other flood prevention measures.

  Here are some steps you can take to protect yourself and your loved ones from the dangers of Hurricane Ian.

Chapter 7

How to make an emergency plan?

Follow these steps to create an emergency plan for Hurricane Ian.

 1. Know your shelter: Evacuation sites can be found on your local emergency management office's website.

2. Identify evacuation routes and emergency evacuation sites: Plan multiple routes in case one route is cut off. Identify a shelter in your area and plan how to get there.

3. Create an emergency kit with food, water, and other essentials: The kit must contain enough food and water for each person in the household to last at least 3 days. You should also bring other essentials such as a first aid kit, flashlight, batteries, radio, and medication. 4. Make a plan for your pet: If evacuation is required, pet care arrangements must be made.

5. Make a plan for communicating with family and friends during a storm: Cell phone service can be disrupted during a hurricane, so it's important to have a backup plan for communications.

6. Be prepared for power outages: Prepare a flashlight, batteries, and radio in case of a power outage.

7. Be prepared for flooding: If you live in a flood-prone area, bring sandbags and other flood prevention measures.

8. Practise your emergency plan with your family: This will help identify potential problems and ensure everyone knows what to do in the event of a hurricane.

  Here are some additional tips for creating an emergency plan:

• Involve the whole family in the planning process.

• This ensures everyone's needs are met and everyone is on the same page. • Please consider the needs of the entire family, including children, the elderly and the disabled.

• Update your emergency plan regularly.

• Needs may change over time. Therefore, it is important to ensure that your emergency plan is up to date. By following these steps, you can create an emergency plan to keep you and your family safe during Hurricane Ian.

Chapter 8

What to pack in your emergency bag

Here is a list of items to pack in your emergency bag for Hurricane Ian.

• Food and Water: Please provide each person in your household with at least enough food and water for her 3 days. Choose shelf-stable foods that don't require cooking or refrigeration. You should also carry at least 1 gallon of water per person per day.

• First aid kit: Pack a first aid kit with basic medical supplies such as bandages, antibiotic ointment, painkillers, and disinfectant wipes.

• Flashlight and Batteries: Please have a flashlight and batteries available in case of a power outage.

• Radio: Bring a battery-operated or hand-crank radio to stay informed about the storm and receive emergency alerts.

• Medications: Pack any medications you or your family may need.

• Important Documents: Pack important documents such as insurance policies, ID cards, and bank documents.

• Other important items: Other items you may want to include in your emergency bag include:

* Change of clothes is limited to once per person.

* One sleeping bag or blanket per person

* A manual can opener.

* Whistle or other signalling device

* Dust mask

* Solar charger

* Multi-tool

* Knife

* Lighter or matches

* Toilet paper and other hygiene products

* Cash

  Additional items can also be packed according to your specific needs. For example, if you have pets, you should also provide food and water for them. If you have a baby, you'll need diapers, wipes, and formula.

  It is important to store your emergency bag in a safe and easily accessible place. Also, be sure to regularly refill your emergency bag with fresh food and water.

  Having an emergency bag on hand will ensure you and your family have the supplies you need to stay safe during Hurricane Ian.

Chapter 9

How to protect your home and property?

Here are some tips to protect your home and property from Hurricane Ian.

- Before the storm •

- Ensure your home is safe.

- Board up windows and doors and cut down trees and branches that could fall and damage your home. If you have time, you can also equip your property with sandbags to protect it from flooding.

- Make a plan for your pet.

- If evacuation is required, pet care arrangements must be made.

- Make a plan for communicating with family and friends during a storm.

- Cell phone service can be disrupted during a hurricane, so it's important to have a backup plan for communications.

- Be prepared for power outages.

- Prepare a flashlight, batteries, and radio in case of a power outage.

- Be prepared for flooding.

- If you live in an area that is prone to flooding, have sandbags or other flood protection measures in place.

- During the storm •

- If you are ordered to evacuate, do so immediately.

- Do not delay evacuating until it is too late.

- If you are unable to evacuate, stay indoors and go to a room on the lowest level of your home.

- If your home has a basement, go to the basement.

- Stay away from windows and doors.

- Listen to the radio for updates on the storm.

• After the storm •

• Do not go outside until the storm has completely passed.

• Check for damage to your home and property.

• If your home is damaged, contact your insurance company to file a claim.

• Stay informed about the latest information on recovery efforts.

Here are some additional tips for protecting your home and property from Hurricane Ian:

• Inspect your roof and make any necessary repairs.

• A damaged roof can be a major source of damage during a hurricane.

• Clean your gutters and downspouts.

• This will help to prevent water from pooling on your roof and causing damage. • Cut down any trees or branches that could fall and cause damage to your home.

• Secure loose items in your yard, such as patio furniture and lawn equipment.

• Store your belongings in areas that are prone to flooding.

• Get flood insurance.

• Flood insurance is not covered by your homeowner's insurance policy, so it is important to purchase it separately.

These steps will help protect your home and property from Hurricane His Ian.

Chapter 10

Where would you go if you needed to evacuate?

When I had to evacuate because of Hurricane Ian, I went to the nearest shelter. Emergency shelters are located in secure buildings and have trained staff who can provide assistance.

To find an emergency shelter near you, visit your local emergency management office's website. To find emergency shelter, you can also call the Federal Emergency Management Agency (FEMA) at 1-800-621-FEMA (3362).

If you cannot evacuate to a shelter, you can stay with friends and family who live in a safe location. You can also stay in hotels and motels.

It is important to note that you should only evacuate if ordered to do so by local authorities. Evacuation is dangerous and it is important to follow the instructions of local authorities.

Here are some tips to help you evacuate safely.

- Make a plan.

- Know where you want to go and how to get there.

- Prepare your emergency kit.

- Kits must include food, water, first aid supplies, and other essentials.

- Stay up to date.

- Listen to the radio or watch the news to stay up to date on the storm.

- Be prepared to wait.

• It may take some time to evacuate everyone. Therefore, be prepared to wait at a shelter or with friends and family.

 Following these tips will help you stay safe during your evacuation.

Chapter 11

How to stay safe during a hurricane?

Here are some tips to stay safe during a hurricane.

• Before the storm •

• Make a plan.

• Know where to go and how to get there if you need to evacuate.

• Prepare your emergency kit.

• Kits must include food, water, first aid supplies, and other essentials.

• Ensure your home is safe.

• Board up windows and doors and cut down trees and branches that could fall and damage your home. If you have time, you can also equip your property with sandbags to protect it from flooding.

• Make a plan for your pet.

• If evacuation is required, pet care arrangements must be made.

• Make a plan for communicating with family and friends during a storm.

• Cell phone service can be disrupted during a hurricane, so it's important to have a backup plan for communications.

• Be prepared for power outages.

• Prepare a flashlight, batteries, and radio in case of a power outage.

• Be prepared for flooding.

• If you live in a flood-prone area, bring sandbags and other flood prevention measures.

• During the storm •

• If you are ordered to evacuate, evacuate immediately.

• Do not postpone evacuation until it is too late.

• If you cannot evacuate, stay indoors and go to the lowest room in your home. • If your home has a basement, go to it. • Stay away from windows and doors.

• Listen to storm updates on the radio.

• After the storm •

• Do not go outside until the storm has completely passed.

• Check your home and property for damage.

• If your home is damaged, please contact your insurance company to file a claim.

• Stay up to date on recovery efforts.

Here are some additional tips to stay safe during a hurricane.

• Avoid driving in flooded areas.

• Even just 6 inches of water can throw you off your feet.

- Be careful of cutting power lines.

- Downed power lines can be fatal. If you find a downed power line, move away from it and call authorities.

- Be careful when using a generator.

- Generators can produce carbon monoxide, a deadly gas. Never run a generator indoors or in a garage.

- Please follow instructions from local authorities.

- Local authorities have the latest information about hurricanes and how to stay safe.

By following these tips, you can protect yourself and your loved ones during a hurricane.

Chapter 12

What should I do if I'm stuck at home during a hurricane?

If you're stuck at home during a hurricane, the most important thing is to stay safe. Here are some tips:

- Go to the lowest floor of the house, preferably the basement.

- This is the safest place to be during a hurricane.

- Stay away from windows and doors.

- Hurricanes can produce strong winds and flying debris that can break windows and doors and cause injuries.

- Listen to the radio to get the latest information about the storm.

- This will help you stay informed and know what to do.

- If you have a generator, please use it safely.

- Generators can produce carbon monoxide, a deadly gas. Never run a generator indoors or in a garage.

If your home floods, you should evacuate as soon as possible. If you are unable to evacuate, you should remain in the highest part of your home and wait for the water to recede.

Here are some additional tips to stay safe if you're stuck at home during a hurricane.

- Make a plan.

- Decide where you will go in your home if the storm gets worse.

- Provide a way to communicate with family and friends.

- Cell phone service may be interrupted during a hurricane. Therefore, have a backup plan for communication.

- Be prepared for power outages.

- Prepare a flashlight, batteries, and radio in case of a power outage.

- Be prepared for flooding.

- If you live in a flood-prone area, bring sandbags and other flood prevention measures.

- Prepare a first aid kit.

- This is useful for treating minor injuries.

If you are stuck at home during a hurricane, it is important to remain calm and follow the instructions of local authorities. By following these tips, you can protect yourself and your loved ones.

Chapter 13

How to recover from a hurricane?

Recovery from a hurricane can be a long and difficult process, but it's important to be patient and remain positive. Here are some tips:

• Assess the damage to your home and property.

• Once the storm has passed, take a walk around your home to assess the damage. This will help you determine what needs to be repaired or replaced.

• Submit a claim to your insurance company.

• If your home or property is insured, file a claim with your insurance company as soon as possible. The insurance company will send an adjuster to evaluate the damage and determine the amount of compensation.

• Begin Repairs •

Once your insurance claim has been approved, you can begin repairs to your home or property. If possible, you can also perform the repairs yourself. However, if the damage is severe, you may need to call a professional.

• Apply for government assistance.

• There are many government programs that can help people affected by hurricanes. You may be eligible for financial assistance, housing assistance, and other types of assistance.

• Get help from volunteers.

• There are many volunteers who are willing to help people recover from a hurricane. You can find volunteers through your local emergency management office or through a volunteer organisation such as the Red Cross or the Salvation Army.

Here are some additional tips for recovering from a hurricane:

• Be patient •

Recovery from a hurricane takes time. It is important to be patient and to stay positive.

• Ask for help.

• Don't be afraid to ask for help from your family, friends, neighbours, or the government. There are people who are willing to help you get back on your feet.

• Take care of yourself.

• It is important to take care of yourself during the recovery process. This means getting enough sleep, eating healthy foods, and exercising regularly. It also means taking time for yourself to relax and de-stress.

Recovering from a hurricane can be challenging, but it is important to remember that you are not alone. There are many people who can help you get back on your feet.

Chapter 14

How to assess damage to your home and property?

Follow these steps to assess damage to your home and property from Hurricane Ian.

1. Inspect the exterior of the house and grounds: Check for damage to the roof, siding, windows, doors, gutters, downspouts, and other exterior areas. You should also check for fallen trees or branches that could be causing damage to your home or property. [Image of inspecting the outside of your home or property for damage caused by a hurricane]

2. Inspect the inside of the house: Look for water damage, such as wet floors, walls, and ceilings. You should also check for damage to appliances, furniture, and other items. [Image of inspecting the inside of a house for damage caused by a hurricane]

3. Take photos and videos of the damage: This will help you record the damage and file a claim with your insurance company. [Photos and video images of hurricane damage]

4. Contact your insurance company: Once you have identified damage to your home or property, contact your insurance company to file a claim. The insurance company will send an adjuster to evaluate the damage and determine the amount of compensation. [Image of contacting insurance company for hurricane compensation claim]

Here are some additional tips for assessing damage to your home and property from Hurricane Ian.

• Please be careful when inspecting your home or property. There may be dangers such as cut power lines or broken glass.
• If you are unsure whether it is safe to enter your home or property, contact your local emergency management office. • Record all costs associated with damage to your home or property. This includes the cost of repairs, replacements, and temporary accommodation.

• Please be careful about insurance. It may take some time for your claim to be processed and payment received.

If you have questions or concerns about assessing damage to your home or property from Hurricane Ian, please contact your local emergency management office or insurance company.

Chapter 15

How to make an insurance claim?

To file an insurance claim, follow these steps:

1. Contact your insurance company: You can usually contact your insurance company by phone, email, or online.

2. Enter your policy number and billing details: This includes the date and time of the loss, the cause of the loss, and the extent of the loss.

3. Please submit your insurance claim form: Your insurance company will provide you with a claim form to fill out. This form requests information about loss, damage, and insurance policies.

4. Please provide documentation to support your claim: This may include photos or videos of damage, receipts for repairs or replacements, and contractor estimates.

5. Work with insurance adjusters: Insurance adjusters investigate claims and assess damages. You should work with the adjuster to provide all the necessary information.

Once the insurance adjuster completes their investigation, the insurance company will decide how much to compensate you. After that, the insurance company will pay the insurance claim.

Here are some additional tips for filing an insurance claim.

• Be honest and accurate when providing information to your insurance company.

• Please keep copies of all documents submitted to the insurance company.

• be patient. It may take some time for your claim to be processed and payment received.

 If you have any questions or concerns regarding your insurance claim, please contact your insurance company.

 Here are some additional tips for filing a hurricane insurance claim.

• Please contact your insurance company immediately after a hurricane occurs. This speeds up the claims process.

• Be prepared to provide your insurance company with information about the hurricane, including B. Hurricane date, time, wind speed, and storm surge.

• Be prepared to provide your insurance company with information about damage to your home and property. This may include photos or videos of the damage, receipts for repairs or replacements, and quotes from contractors.

• be patient. It may take some time for the insurance company to process your claim and for you to receive payment.

 If you have any questions or concerns about filing an insurance claim for hurricane damage, please contact your insurance company.

Chapter 16

How to get help from FEMA and other organisations?

There are several ways to receive assistance from FEMA and other organisations after Hurricane Ian.

• FEMA •

To receive assistance from FEMA, you can:

- Apply online at DisasterAssistance.gov

- Call the FEMA Helpline at 1-800-621-FEMA (3362).

- Use the FEMA mobile app

When you apply for FEMA assistance, you must provide information about your household, income, and damage to your home and property.

• Other organisations •

There are many other organisations that can provide assistance after Hurricane Ian. These organisations include, but are not limited to:

- American Red Cross

- Salvation Army

- unified path

- Human Habitat

- Volunteers from America

Find contact information for these organisations online or by calling your local emergency management office.

In addition to FEMA and other organisations, there are many other ways to receive assistance after Hurricane Ian. You can:

• Ask family and friends for help.

• Please contact your nearest emergency management office.

• Please contact the person in charge of your local government.

• Contact local religious and community groups.

There are many people and organisations who can help you after Hurricane Ian. Don't be afraid to ask for help.

Here are some additional tips for getting help from FEMA and other organisations after Hurricane Ian.

• be patient. After a hurricane, you may experience a high volume of calls and applications. It may take some time to get help.

• Stay organised. When applying for FEMA assistance or seeking assistance from other organisations, be sure to have all your information ready. This will help speed up the process.

• Be persistent. Don't give up if you don't get help right away. Keep trying until you get the help you need. Remember you are not alone. There are many people who can help you after Hurricane Ian.

Chapter 17

Lessons learned from Hurricane Ian

Hurricane Ian was a powerful and destructive storm that caused significant damage and loss of life. Below are some of the lessons learned from Hurricane Ian.

• Evacuation is very important.

• If you are ordered to evacuate, evacuate immediately. Do not delay evacuation until it is too late.

• Be prepared for power outages.

• Prepare a flashlight, batteries, and radio in case of a power outage.

• Be prepared for flooding.

• If you live in a flood-prone area, bring sandbags and other flood prevention measures.

• Please follow instructions from local authorities.

• Local officials have the latest information about the storm and how to stay safe.

 In addition to these general lessons, there are many other lessons that can be learned from Hurricane Ian. For example:

• Infrastructure needs to be more resilient to storms.

• Many of the power outages and flooding during Hurricane Ian were caused by infrastructure damage. Infrastructure needs to be more storm resistant to withstand high winds and flooding.

• Climate change is making storms more intense.

• Hurricane Ian was a Category 4 hurricane when it made landfall. Climate change is making storms more intense, so we need to prepare for more powerful hurricanes in the future.

• We need to invest in mitigation measures.

• Mitigation measures, such as raising homes and building seawalls, can help reduce damage from storms. We must invest in mitigation measures to protect our communities from storms.

  Hurricane Ian was a devastating storm, but it's important to learn from it to prepare for future storms. By taking steps to prepare for a storm, we can protect ourselves, our loved ones, and our communities.

Chapter 18

Preparing for the next hurricane

To prepare for the next hurricane, you can take the following steps:

• Before the storm •

• Know your evacuation zones and plan where to go if you need to evacuate.

• Evacuation zones can be found on your local emergency management agency's website.

• Create an emergency kit containing food, water, and other essentials.

• Kits must contain enough food and water for at least 3 days for each person in the household. You should also bring other essentials such as a first aid kit, flashlight, batteries, radio, and medication. • Keep your home and property safe.

• Board up windows and doors and cut down trees and branches that could fall and damage your home. If you have time, you can also equip your property with sandbags to protect it from flooding.

• Make a plan for your pet.

• If evacuation is required, pet care arrangements must be made.

• Make a plan for communicating with family and friends during a storm.

• Cell phone service can be disrupted during a hurricane, so it's important to have a backup plan for communications.

• Be prepared for power outages.

• Prepare a flashlight, batteries, and radio in case of a power outage.

• Be prepared for flooding.

• If you live in a flood-prone area, bring sandbags and other flood prevention measures.

• Stay up to date with the latest weather forecasts and warnings from the National Hurricane Centre.

• Check the National Hurricane Centre website or your local news station for the latest weather information.

• During the storm •

• If you are ordered to evacuate, do so immediately.

• Do not delay evacuating until it is too late.

• If you are unable to evacuate, stay indoors and go to a room on the lowest level of your home.

• If your home has a basement, go to the basement.

• Stay away from windows and doors.

• Listen to the radio for updates on the storm.

• After the storm •

• Do not go outside until the storm has completely passed.

• Check for damage to your home and property.

• If your home is damaged, contact your insurance company to file a claim.

• Stay informed about the latest information on recovery efforts.

In addition to these steps, you can also prepare for the next hurricane by:

• Learning about the different types of hurricanes and how they form.

• This will help you to better understand the risks and to make informed decisions about how to prepare.

• Making a hurricane preparedness plan for your family and business.

• This plan should include information on evacuation, communication, and recovery. • Staying informed about the latest hurricane forecasts and warnings.

• This will help you to be prepared for a hurricane even if it is not expected to make landfall in your area. By taking these steps, you can protect yourself and your loved ones from the next hurricane.

Chapter 19

Hurricane Ian Case Study: Stories of those affected by the storm

Hurricane Ian was a powerful and destructive storm that caused significant damage and loss of life. Here are some stories from people affected by the storm.

• Fort Myers Beach family lost everything •

Her family of four, living in Fort Myers Beach, lost their home and all their possessions to Hurricane Ian. The storm surge reached 12 feet in her neighbourhood, completely destroying her home. The family was able to reach safety, but now faces the difficult task of rebuilding their lives.

• An elderly couple left behind at home •

An elderly Fort Myers couple was stranded in their home during Hurricane Ian. The storm surge flooded his house and he was unable to get out. After the storm passed, the couple was rescued by paramedics, but both were hospitalised with injuries.

• Manager who lost everything •

A Punta Gorda business owner lost his business and everything he worked for in the aftermath of Hurricane Ian. The storm surge destroyed his building and all its inventory. The owner is currently unemployed and struggling to make ends meet. These are just a few of the many stories of people affected by Hurricane Ian. The storm caused billions of dollars in damage and left thousands of people homeless. Recovery efforts continue, but it will take months, if not years, for the area to fully recover.

In addition to the stories above, here are some other stories from people affected by Hurricane Ian.

• Families who lost a pet •

A Punta Gorda family lost their beloved dog in Hurricane Ian. The dog was washed away by the storm surge and the family was never able to find it.

• Volunteers who lost their lives •

A volunteer helping with hurricane relief efforts was killed by a tree. The volunteer was a father of two, and his death was a tragic reminder of the dangers of working in disaster areas.

• A community gathered •

Despite the damage caused by Hurricane Ian, the community has come together to support each other. Volunteers came from all over the country to help with clean up and recovery efforts. Local businesses will donate food, water and other supplies. And Floridians have shown resilience and strength in the face of tragedy.

Although Hurricane Ian was a devastating storm, it is important to remember that it is also a story of hope and resilience. Floridians are strong and determined to rebuild their lives and communities.

Chapter 20

Hurricane preparedness tips for specific populations, including seniors, people with disabilities, and pets

Here are some hurricane preparedness tips for specific populations, such as the elderly, people with disabilities, and pets.

• senior citizen •

• Be sure to have an evacuation plan in place.

• If you need to evacuate, plan where you are going and how you will get there. We recommend registering with your local emergency management agency's special needs registry.

• Make a plan for communicating with family and friends during the storm.

• Cell phone service may be interrupted. Therefore, have a backup plan for communication.

• Make sure you have enough food, water, and medicine.

• Emergency kits should contain at least three days' worth of food and water, as well as necessary medications.

• Please be aware of the risk of flooding. • If you live in a flood-prone area, bring sandbags and other flood prevention measures.

• Be prepared for power outages.

• Prepare a flashlight, batteries, and radio in case of a power outage.

• People with disabilities •

• Be sure to have an evacuation plan in place.

• If you need to evacuate, plan where you are going and how you will get there. We recommend registering with your local emergency management agency's special needs registry.

• Make a plan for communicating with family and friends during the storm.

• Cell phone service may be interrupted. Therefore, have a backup plan for communication.

• Make sure you have enough food, water, and medicine.

• Emergency kits should contain at least three days' worth of food and water, as well as necessary medications.

• Please be aware of the risk of flooding. • If you live in a flood-prone area, bring sandbags and other flood prevention measures.

• Be prepared for power outages.

• Prepare a flashlight, batteries, and radio in case of a power outage.

• Pets •

• Be sure to have a plan for your pet.

• If you need to evacuate, please make arrangements for pet care. You may consider leaving your pet in a kennel or looking for a pet-friendly hotel.

• Get a pet emergency response kit.

• Your pet's emergency response kit should include food, water, bowl, leash, collar, and any necessary medications for your pet.

• Make sure your pet has an ID.

• Pets must have a collar with their name and contact information. You may also want to consider implanting a microchip in your pet.

 In addition to these general tips, here are some additional tips for specific populations.

• senior citizen •

• Watch for signs of heat exhaustion or heat stroke.

• Heat exhaustion and heat stroke can be serious illnesses, especially for the elderly. If you feel dizzy, lightheaded, nausea, or feverish, move to a cool area and drink plenty of fluids. If cooling is not possible, seek medical attention immediately.

• Make a plan to stay hydrated.

• Staying hydrated during a hurricane is especially important for older adults. Even if you're not thirsty, make sure you have enough water on hand to stay hydrated throughout the day.

• Be aware of the risk of falling.

• Falls are a major risk factor for injury and death in older adults. Proceed carefully and use handrails and other aids as necessary.

• People with disabilities •

• Make sure your emergency preparedness kit includes all necessary items.

• This may include wheelchairs, walkers, canes, and other equipment.

• Have a plan for getting to your evacuation destination.

• If you need assistance getting to your evacuation destination, contact your local emergency management office.

• Be aware of your rights and resources.

• You have the right to be treated equally and to have access to the resources you need. If you feel that your rights are being violated, contact an advocacy organisation or your local emergency management office.

• Pets •

• Make sure your pet is up-to-date on their vaccinations.

• This will help to protect them from diseases that may be more common during a hurricane.

• Be aware of the risks of heat exhaustion and heat stroke.

• Heat exhaustion and heat stroke can be serious medical conditions, especially for pets. Make sure your pet has access to fresh water and shade at all times. If you are concerned that your pet may be suffering from heat exhaustion or heat stroke, seek veterinary attention immediately.

• Be prepared for stress and anxiety.

• Hurricanes can be stressful and anxiety-inducing for pets. Make sure your pet has a safe and comfortable place to stay during the hurricane. You may also want to consider talking to your veterinarian about medication or other ways to help your pet cope with stress and anxiety.

  By following these tips, you can help to protect yourself, your loved ones, and your pets during a hurricane.

Chapter 21

List of resources for hurricane relief and recover

Here is a list of resources for hurricane relief and recovery.

• Federal Emergency Management Agency (FEMA): FEMA provides assistance to individuals and communities affected by natural disasters. You can apply for FEMA assistance online at DisasterAssistance.gov, by calling the FEMA Helpline at 1-800-621-FEMA (3362), or by using the FEMA mobile app.

• American Red Cross: The American Red Cross provides a variety of services to people affected by disasters, including food, shelter, and emotional support. Contact the Red Cross at 1-800-RED-CROSS (733-2767) or visit RedCross.org.

Salvation Army: The Salvation Army provides food, shelter, and other assistance to people affected by disasters. To contact the Salvation Army, call 1-800-SAL-ARMY (1-800-725-2769) or visit the website SalvationArmyUSA.org.

United Way: United Way is a network of local organisations that provide a variety of services to people in need. Contact information for your local United Way can be found on the UnitedWay.org website.

Habitat for Humanity: Habitat for Humanity helps people build and repair homes. Contact Habitat for Humanity at 1-800-HABITAT (1-800-422-4828) or visit the website Habitat.org.

Volunteers of America: Volunteers of America provides a variety of services to people in need, including food, housing, and job training. Contact Volunteers of America at 1-800-USA-VOLS (1-800-872-8657) or visit the website VolunteersOfAmerica.org.

 In addition to these national agencies, there are a number of local agencies that provide hurricane relief and recovery services. Contact information for local organisations can be found by contacting your local emergency management office or by searching online.

 If you're looking for a way to help those affected by the hurricane, please donate or volunteer your time and skills to one of the organisations listed above. There are many ways to volunteer.

For example: B. Clearing debris, distributing food and water, or providing emotional support.

 Every little bit helps, so please consider donating your time or volunteering to help those affected by the hurricane.

www.ingramcontent.com/pod-product-compliance
Lightning Source LLC
Chambersburg PA
CBHW040309240726

48664CB00006B/1436